D0635898

Moses in the Bulrushes

Series editor: Rachel Cooke
Art director: Robert Walster
Consultants: Reverend Richard Adfield,
Laurie Rosenberg, The Board of Deputies of British Jews

First published in 1999 by Franklin Watts

First American edition 1999 by Franklin Watts
A Division of Grolier Publishing
90 Sherman Turnpike
Danbury, CT 06816

Visit Franklin Watts on the Internet at:
http://publishing.grolier.com

ISBN 0-531-14516-6 (lib. bdg.) 0-531-15387-8 (pbk.)

A CIP catalog record for this book is
available from the Library of Congress

Text copyright © Franklin Watts 1999
Illustrations copyright © Diana Mayo 1999
Printed in Hong Kong/China

Moses in the Bulrushes

Retold by Mary Auld
Illustrated by Diana Mayo

W
FRANKLIN WATTS
A Division of Grolier Publishing
NEW YORK • LONDON • HONG KONG • SYDNEY
DANBURY, CONNECTICUT

There once was a Hebrew named Jacob, whom God had named Israel. He and his family had come to Egypt to live with his son Joseph, who was chief adviser to Pharaoh, king of Egypt. After Jacob and his sons died, their families continued to grow, and the Children of Israel spread throughout the land of Egypt.

Now a new Pharaoh became king. He was worried by the Israelites. "We must control their numbers or they may join our enemies and fight us in war," he warned. So the Egyptians made the Israelites their slaves and forced them to work for them. Yet their numbers continued to grow.

The Egyptians began to fear the
Israelites. They treated them cruelly
and worked them still harder.
Pharaoh even ordered the midwives,
who helped at the birth of Hebrew
children, to kill any baby boys that
were born. But the midwives feared

God and did not do as Pharaoh
asked. The number of Israelites still
continued to grow.

Now Pharaoh made a terrible
decision. He ordered his people to
throw every boy baby born to the
Israelites into the River Nile.

At this time, a certain man and woman among the Israelites married, and, in due course, had a baby son. The woman looked at her baby—he was beautiful. How could she kill him? For three months, she hid him at home.

When she could no longer keep the boy safely hidden, she found a wicker basket and coated it with tar and pitch. She put her son in the basket and left it among the bulrushes at the edge of the Nile. Some way off, her daughter watched to see what would happen.

Pharaoh's daughter came down to the Nile to bathe that day, while her attendants walked along the bank. So it was she who first spotted the basket among the reeds and ordered her slave girl to fetch it. Pharaoh's daughter opened up the basket and found the baby crying inside. She felt

great pity for the boy. "This must be a Hebrew child," she said.

Now the boy's sister came forward: "Shall I fetch a Hebrew nurse to look after the baby?" she offered, and when Pharaoh's daughter agreed, she rushed straight to her mother and brought her to the riverside.

"Take this child and nurse it for me," said Pharaoh's daughter. "I shall pay you a good wage."

And the woman took back her baby and nursed him at her home.

When the boy was old enough, his mother took him to the palace. Pharaoh's daughter adopted the child and made him her son. "I shall call him Moses," she said, which means "drawn from the water."

Moses grew to be a man in the court of the Egyptians, but he did not forget his true family. One day, as he watched a group of Hebrews laboring, he saw an Egyptian beating one of them. Thinking no one was watching, Moses killed the Egyptian and buried his body in the sand.

The next day, he saw two Hebrews fighting each other. He tried to stop them, but they just said, "Who are you to tell us to stop fighting? Will you kill us as you killed the Egyptian?"

Moses was frightened. People knew about the murder, and as soon as Pharaoh heard of it, he would want Moses dead, too. So Moses ran away, leaving Egypt for the land of Midian.

Moses was sitting exhausted by a
well when the seven daughters of the
priest of Midian came to draw water
for their sheep and goats. Some
shepherds drove the girls away, but
Moses took their side, and then helped
them to give water to their flock.

16

To thank Moses, the girls' father, Jethro, invited him to stay. Moses was happy to find a home. Even better, the priest gave Moses his daughter Zipporah as a wife. Soon they had a son and named him Gershom, which meant "stranger." "For I have been a stranger in a foreign land," said Moses.

While Moses tended his father-in-law's flock in Midian, the Israelites in Egypt continued to suffer. There was a new king, but he was just as harsh as the old one. The Children of Israel were groaning under the weight of their slavery, and they cried to God for help. And God heard them.

One day, Moses drove his sheep into
the wilderness and onto the slopes of
Horeb, the mountain of God. There he
saw a strange sight: a bush on fire. But
although the flames burned brightly,
the bush was not burned up by them.
Moses turned to have a better look.

As he did so, a voice called out to him from the bush, "Moses! Moses!"

"Here I am," replied Moses.

"Do not come any closer, but take off your sandals, for you are standing on holy ground," commanded the voice. "I am God, the God of your fathers, the God of Abraham, Isaac, and Jacob."

Moses was afraid and hid his face—he did not want to look upon God.

"I have come to take my people, the Children of Israel, away from slavery," God continued. "I shall take them out of Egypt to a new land—a land flowing with milk and honey. You must go to Pharaoh for me now so that you can lead my people out of Egypt."

Moses was amazed. "Who am I that you should ask me to do such a thing?"

"I shall be with you," replied God. "You will speak in my name."

"When I go to my people, what name should I give you?" asked Moses.

"I am who I am," replied God. "Tell them 'I am' has sent you to them."

And God explained to Moses what he should do: how he must tell the Israelites of God's promise and how he should ask Pharaoh to let the Israelites travel into the desert to worship God.

And God gave Moses three signs to show his power. First, he told Moses to throw his wooden staff on the ground. Instantly, it became a snake, but when Moses picked it up by its tail, the snake became a staff once more.

Second, God told Moses to put his hand inside his cloak and draw it out again. When he did this, Moses found his hand had become diseased and covered in white scales, like snow. He put his hand back inside his cloak and drew it out again. His hand was healthy once more.

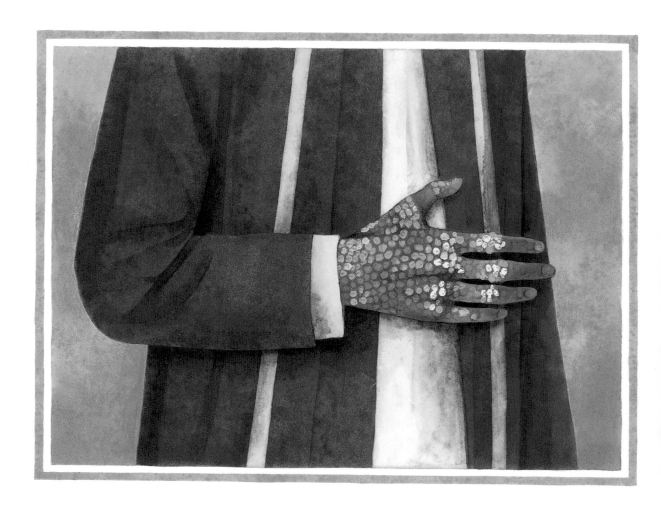

"If they don't believe either of these signs," said God, "then here is a third: take water from the Nile and pour it on the ground. It will turn into blood."

Moses was still worried: "Even with these signs, I am not good at speaking and arguing with people."

"Didn't I give you your mouth and tongue? I will help you speak and teach you what to say," said God.

But Moses said, "Lord, please ask someone else to do it."

God became angry. "Your brother Aaron will speak for you. He is on his way to meet you. You will be to him as I am to you—you will tell him what to say. And you will carry the staff so you can perform the signs."

Moses returned to his wife and her family. "Let me go back to my own people in Egypt to see how they are," he asked his father-in-law, Jethro.

"Go in peace," Jethro replied.

So Moses set out for Egypt once more with his family. In his hand he carried God's staff. He realized now why he had been saved from the bulrushes all those years ago. He was the one whom God had chosen to free the Israelites from slavery. One day, he hoped, he would bring them to the land flowing with milk and honey, the good land that God had promised.

About This Story

Moses in the Bulrushes is a retelling of part of Exodus, one of the books that make up the Bible—the collection of writings that are sacred, in different forms, to the Christian and Jewish religions. Exodus is the second of 39 books in the Hebrew Bible, Tanakh, or the Christian Old Testament. As one of the first five books of the Bible, Exodus is also part of the Torah, the most sacred text of the Jewish religion.

Who Was Moses?

Moses is one of the most important figures of the Bible and in the history of the Hebrews, the people who began the Jewish religion. He lived at some time between 1350 and 1250 B.C. He had a very close relationship with God, who spoke to him directly throughout his life. Under God's guidance, he not only led the Hebrews out of slavery in Egypt (see below) but also gave them His laws and rules, including the Ten Commandments, which became central to the Jewish faith. These laws are also a key part of Christian belief, but they are approached through the teachings of Jesus.

The Hebrews in Egypt

The Hebrews had come to Egypt to avoid famine in Canaan, perhaps as much as 400 years before Moses's birth. At this stage, they were probably just a large family, headed by Jacob who, called Israel by God, was the son of Isaac and grandson of Abraham. Jacob had twelve sons and one of his sons, Joseph, was already in Egypt. He was in charge of Egypt's grain stores and had invited his family to Egypt with Pharaoh's permission. In the centuries that followed, Jacob's family of descendants, the Children of Israel, grew ever larger, forming a community that, with Moses as their leader, began to think of itself as the Hebrew people.

 28

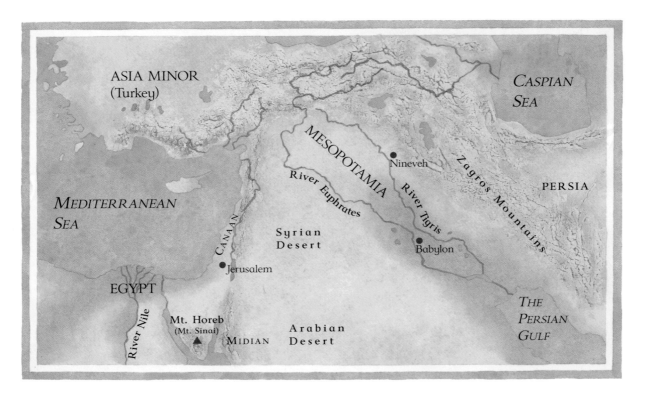

ASIA MINOR
(Turkey)

CASPIAN
SEA

MESOPOTAMIA

Nineveh

Zagros Mountains

PERSIA

MEDITERRANEAN
SEA

River Euphrates

River Tigris

CANAAN

Syrian
Desert

Babylon

Jerusalem

EGYPT

THE
PERSIAN
GULF

River Nile

Mt. Horeb
(Mt. Sinai)

MIDIAN

Arabian
Desert

The Promised Land

Moses in the Bulrushes retells the very beginning of Exodus. Joseph is long
forgotten, and the Hebrews have become the Egyptians' work force, their
slaves. Aware of His people's unhappiness, God chooses Moses to lead them
out of slavery. When He speaks to Moses through the burning bush, he
promises the Hebrews their own land. It is partly this promise of land that
helps the Hebrews see themselves as a people and a "nation."

With God's help, Moses manages to free the Hebrews from Egypt, but
they still have to reach the promised land. For forty years, they wander
through the wilderness. Moses fights to keep the Hebrews together and
trusting in God's promise. Moses never reaches the promised land, Canaan,
although he sees it from a distance before he dies. His great achievement is
to bring his people there, held together by strong laws and their faith in God.

Useful Words

Bulrushes Bulrushes are a type of water plant or reed that grows at the edges of rivers and lakes. The bulrush is part of the sedge family, as is the papyrus plant that grows along the River Nile. It is likely the bulrushes mentioned in the Bible are in fact papyrus.

Hebrew The Hebrews were an ancient people from the Middle East region of Asia. The Jewish religion began among the Hebrews, who are also sometimes called the Children of Israel or the Israelites. Most of the Hebrew Bible was originally written in the Hebrew language.

Holy We say something is holy when it is sacred to God. It is perfect and without fault.

Israelite See *Hebrew*.

Midwives (singular: midwife) Midwives are nurses who look after women when they have a baby. They have special knowledge of childbirth.

Pharaoh Pharaoh is the title given to the kings of ancient Egypt.

Pitch See *Tar*.

Pity Pity is a feeling of sorrow and understanding for another person who is hurt or unhappy or in a difficult situation.

Promise A promise is an undertaking to carry out a task or action at a future date. A promise is not easy to make. If you promise, you are not just saying something; you are saying you really will do it. God's promise to Moses and the Hebrews is that He will lead them out of Egypt and to their own country.

Staff A staff is a long straight, walking stick.

Tar Tar is a black sticky substance extracted from burned wood or coal. Pitch is a similar substance, but shiny. Tar and pitch are waterproof and so can be used to make a container watertight.

Worship To worship God is to praise Him and to show your love for Him. There are many ways of worshiping God, including praying. Christians often worship God by going to services held in a church. Jews worship God at services in a synagogue or at home.

What Do You Think?

These are some questions about *Moses in the Bulrushes* to ask yourself and to talk about with other people:

Why do you think Pharaoh was so worried about the Israelites?

Why do you think the midwives disobeyed Pharaoh's orders?

What did you think about Pharaoh's daughters' decision to adopt Moses?

Why do you think Moses killed the Egyptian slave driver?

Do you think Moses was right to run away from Egypt?

Do you think Moses had ever felt like "a stranger in a foreign land" before he went to Midian?

How do you think Moses felt when God first spoke to him?

Why do you think Moses didn't want to carry out God's request?

Have you ever made a promise? Did you keep it?

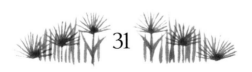